CHRIST & THE WESTERN MIND

LOVE & BELIEF

TRANSLATED BY
EDWARD BULLOUGH, M.A.
FELLOW OF GONVILLE AND CAIUS COLLEGE, CAMBRIDGE

TWO ESSAYS BY
KARL ADAM

CHRIST AND
THE WESTERN MIND

LOVE AND BELIEF

LONDON
SHEED & WARD
1931

NIHIL OBSTAT : INNOCENTIVS APAP, O.P., S.T.D.

CENSOR DEPVTATVS

IMPRIMATVR : EDM : CAN : SVRMONT

VIC. GEN.

WESTMONASTERII, DIE 7ᴬ APRILIS, 1930

1 4 0 2 4

First published April 1930
by Sheed and Ward
from 31 Paternoster Row, London, E.C.4
Second Impression, January 1931

CHRIST AND
THE WESTERN MIND

CHRIST AND THE WESTERN MIND

The subject "Christ and the Western Mind" is in the air and claims attention. Yet it sounds bombastic, aggressive, even impertinent. It has the stilted sound of high-brow literature and strikes anyone anxious for lucid phrases and assured data as repellent and otiose. What does it mean, "East and West," seeing that, besides, there is America, Africa and Australia? And what does "the Western Mind" mean? Is it possible nowadays to speak in all seriousness, with Houston S. Chamberlain and Spengler, of the "Western Mind" as a unitary thing?

The ideas "West," "Western Mind," must, evidently, be used only with great caution; and if, in such circumstances, the subject is to yield any sense, it should perhaps be formulated in the question: Why does Western Europe need Christ and His message? The answer to this question would have to consider the western soul in its make-up, its aims, its needs and necessities, and in view of these to show that these aims and needs can find their ultimate fulfilment and satisfaction only in the belief in Christ.

But I must confess that even this form of the question repels me. It is typical in its western presumption. For if Christ is, as our Faith proclaims, God

7

made Man, the creative Cause, the decisive sense and the only great aim of our existence; if He is the *Kyrios*, the King, to whom we are in the very nature of our being subject, who moreover has redeemed us afresh by His blood—then He and His message cannot be made dependent on western needs in any way, as if He were fulfilling a merely complementary function for Western Europe and its welfare, and as if He, the Logos, were there for no other purpose than to make up for the futilities and stupidities of the western mind; in short, as if He existed for Western Europe and not rather Western Europe for His sake. In point of fact, the situation is this: even if the western mind had no inner needs, if it were still pure nature, unspoilt by philosophy, economics and mechanisation, Christ would still confront it with the peremptory command: *"Sequere me*—follow Me"! Europe stands in relation to Christ, not because it needs Him, but because He gives the order, because He stands before it as a Command. This relation is *a priori*, i.e. it depends in no wise on the approval or good-will of the West, but is imposed before any personal decision, by Christ Himself. Imposed in mercy, certainly; nevertheless imposed! Imposed as early as that white night when the Logos descended upon earth and the light shone from Bethlehem.

If our subject is to bear a Christian meaning and stand the test of our Faith, its question must be, not: "Does the West need Christ and His message?" but:

8

"Why is His message in its full sense addressed precisely to us of the West?" Why are we under a quite special obligation to Him, an obligation such that we destroy not only our supernatural but even our natural life if we abandon Him? Wherein lies, therefore, our peculiar western responsibility towards Christ? Where is the talent that we have to account for until the Master comes? What is our vocation?

I

When the Logos, the second Divine Person, entered this world of space and time, He was, according to the flesh, the son of David, that is, of Jewish descent. Bethlehem, Nazareth, Jerusalem, Golgotha, are all Jewish names. The miracle of Christ was fulfilled within the narrow space of the Jewish world, and the first messengers of His teaching, the Apostles, they too were Jews, Semites, children of the Orient. The Church arose first on Jewish soil; the central point of irradiation of the primitive Christian movement was the Jewish capital, Jerusalem.

Seen from outside, the first Christian community was then a thoroughly Semitic-Jewish product, the fruit of the oriental mind. Yet it was not the East that was the field where the young shoot was to grow into the strong plant, but the West. Here, of course, we must remember that in those days of the growing Christendom the limits of East and West did not wholly coincide with these geographical terms.

Since Asia Minor, Syria, Palestine, Egypt formed parts of the Roman Empire, these countries were in a large measure under the influence of the western, Graeco-Roman civilisation. The frontier of the West was accordingly pushed considerably further East; or rather a sort of intermediate zone had been formed between the pure East and the pure West, in which eastern and western peculiarities permeated each other and produced a new civilisation, the Hellenistic culture. Its characteristic feature was the union of the western *logos* and the eastern *eros*, of western sense of form and eastern vitality. In the West was the home of rationalism, metaphysics, philosophy; the East was the home of irrationalism, mysticism, revelation. But the leading rôle belonged, even in this sphere of Hellenistic culture, to the western mind.

Now, it is characteristic of Christianity that it planted its first cuttings just in this Hellenistic world, this oriental world informed by the western spirit. The first blood spilt for the sake of Christ was that of the Hellenist, St. Stephen. The new honourable name, *Christians*, came into being through the bold witness to "our Lord Christ," not in Jerusalem, but in Antioch. The strongest, most vital churches of the East, those of Asia Minor, of Syria and of Egypt, were without exception Hellenistic. The purely Jewish communities of Palestine and the Diaspora soon died or separated themselves off as various sects. It seemed as if the new plant, obeying some instinct of its primitive nature, needed a soil which had somehow had some western cultivation. We know that this natural instinct of the young Christendom, leading it to the West, was part of God's providence. We therefore know also that the first great mission-field of Christianity was this same West. The new creation gravitated westwards with such force that even the Primate of the Apostles, though destined for the mission among the circumcised, transferred his action from Jerusalem to Rome, and Paul risked his life to cast out Jewish customs from Christianity and became the Apostle of the Greeks. By the time the Apostles died and the inspiration of the New Testament revelation was completed, Christianity had its centre of gravity no longer in the East but in the West.

The fact must, of course, not be overlooked that, just because the first Hellenistic communities grew up in a soil enriched equally by eastern and western civilisations, the East too took its fair share in the spread of Christianity. Perhaps we might say that those who spread it during the first five centuries in the East were most of them men whose head was western, but whose heart was eastern. We shall see later that this oriental element became effective in the special developments of eastern Christianity also. Still, the fact remains that we can speak no longer of a purely oriental Christianity and that even in its eastern form the western traits persisted as predominant. For that reason, too, eastern Christianity began to stagnate and even to decay, the moment western influence was curtailed or completely cut out. It is certain, at any rate, that Christianity was able to give effect to its peculiar impulses, its vivifying creative powers, its leaven, only in the West, which thus remained for two thousand years the real fertile sowing ground of the Christian missions. If at first the harvest was but small, was threatened again and again by the wild storms of persecutions and trampled down, yet it was there. *"Sanguis martyrum semen Christianorum."* The Christian Faith, even though massacred over and over again, was the only vital thing in the decaying Roman Empire ; and when the Germanic tribes broke into the frontiers and combined their youthful vitality and spirit of heroism with the the spirit of Jesus, the dawn of a new day broke for Christendom. It was not long before the cross sparkled on the crown of the Frankish king and soon also on the diadem of the Roman Emperor of the German nation. And at last came the day when the whole of Europe—apart from a few heathenish corners—had become Christian, and the West, however divided in its tongues and split into nations, united in a single sublime sanctity, in the confession of Christ. It was in Christ that the West had found its true unity, more intimate and more subtle than all the ties of blood, stronger and more lasting than any unity imposed by common fate: the unity of the same faith and the same worship. It was only then that the western soul came into being. It was born from the common possession of the Flesh and Blood of Christ. He became then for centuries the heart of the West, its home, its wealth, its all: Head and Body were one Christ.

2

The fruitful results of the outward contacts between the message of Christ and the spirit of the West found its correspondence in their inner relations. The call of Christ went out to the West not only in the sense that it was obediently to accept His word, but also that it was to help actively in the building of the new temple of God that was rising from its foundations. It was a call to place its peculiar genius at the service of Christ.

These relations must, of course, not be misunderstood as meaning that thereby the message of Christ had been given a new substance, or implying a fusion between the spirit of Christ and the spirit of the West. The word of Christ, on the contrary, remained identically the same throughout the centuries, the word of the Logos, strictly supernatural, transcendent, a message from on high, protected against all error by the Apostolic office and the power of the Holy Ghost which had been promised to that office. What gave Christianity its immense driving-force, though also its stigma of blood and wounds, was precisely that it entered and passed through the world not as a piece of human wisdom but as something utterly different, as the tremendous

13

paradox, the *scandalum crucis* which wearies the wisdom of the wise and comes as a gift to the childlike faith. Christian revelation, the mystery of the crucified God, was and is something whole and complete, ended by the death of the last apostle, even though the entire content of its truth may not be explicitly displayed in all its fullness, but lies nestling like a closed bud in the Church's consciousness of her revealing power. It is therefore not in the sense of new truths acquired that we speak of the contribution of the western mind to Christianity, but simply of their formulation and application in the specific manner corresponding to the western spirituality, and of the specifically western form of their inner actualisation. In this sense it is the western mind that it has pleased Divine Providence to call to render labourer's service for the building of the royal edifice of Christian truth. To be sure, this service was never rendered otherwise than under the visible direction of the ecclesiastical *magisterium* and under the invisible guidance of the Holy Ghost; still, it was a service rendered by the forces of the peculiarly western mind, so that, in that sense at least, we may speak of a specifically western form of Christianity. From this point of view, nothing could be more perverse than Houston Stewart Chamberlain's misguided remark in his book, *The Foundations of the Nineteenth Century:* "As crippled helots of the Jews we drag ourselves along behind Jahve's Ark." It is not Jewish wisdom, but the eternal truth of God that is the pearl

14

greeting us with its radiance in the gospel of Christ. And this imperishable pearl is borne in a western setting. Perhaps we might, with great caution, venture to say: As the historical Jesus bore the shape of a son of David, so the form of the mystical Christ is western.

It must suffice to have indicated in these short remarks these formal influences of the western spirit upon the shaping of ecclesiastical Christendom. Even in the Gospel a western note becomes audible, for instance, when St. John expresses the Divine mystery of the Son of Man by means of the Platonic-Stoical term *Logos*, or when he translates the Semitic ideas of "the Kingdom of Heaven," the "Kingdom of God" by the words "Truth" and "Life." The long series of the Apologists and Church Fathers followed the practice of St. John, from Justin to the Cappadocians down to St. Augustine and St. John Damascene. They all took the "gold of the Egyptians" with them on their pilgrimage to the promised land of Faith. In the early times of Christianity, when the central truths of the creation of the world and the eternal generation of the Logos occupied the faithful thinkers, it was Plato from whom they learnt. His view of the world as a rational whole, his doctrine of the κόσμος νοητός, of the unchanging ideas and their creative power, of the illumination of the human mind, provided not only the necessary bridge between faith and intellect, but helped also towards a deeper, more fundamental consideration of the problem presented by revelation, and furnished formulae that expressed its cognisable elements so precisely as to render heretical misinterpretations impossible. It is not surprising to encounter Plato or at any rate his successors, disciples and friends of the neo-Platonic school, not only in the forecourts of Christianity, but right in its mysteries, in the trinitarian and christo-logical speculations. It was especially in the spirit of Origen and St. Augustine that Plato seemed to have a Christian rebirth. When later at the opening of the twelfth century the mind of the West began to turn towards Aristotle, and the approaching forces of a monistically-minded Aristotelianism threatened wes-tern thought, Thomas Aquinas appeared, the gifted pupil of a great master. By combining Aristotelianism with the most essential elements of Platonic thought and adjusting it to Christian truths, he brought it into the service of the Cross of Christ. Despite all opposition he pressed the intellectual weapons of Aristotelianism so completely into Christ's service that even to-day the theologian can hardly move a step without keeping his eye fixed on St. Thomas and the Philosopher of Stagira. Nor was it only certain terms of scholastic thought that he embedded in the structure of Christian theology, such as *matter* and *form*, *substance* and *accident*, *potency* and *act*, but entire ranges of thought, like the Aristotelian conception of science, the Aristotelian theory of knowledge, the metaphysics of being, were translated by him into a Christian form.

While thus Christian thought displays Greek elements, the Christian ordering of conduct, the practice of ecclesiastical life in western Christendom, bears a markedly Roman colouring. The *imperium romanum* itself provided by its very existence and by being what it was, a natural model which the Church of Christ could, and did, in fact, use for the execution of its supernatural task. "Grace presupposes nature"; that applies also to the building and expansion of the Papal Church. The call of St. Peter to be the Rock of the Church and the guardian of the Keys, and the erection of the Church of Rome as the *cathedra Petri* and *ecclesia principalis* had their natural presupposition and basis in the unique historical position of Rome with its preeminent authority as mistress of nations. When St. Peter, under the impulse of the Holy Ghost, went to Rome, he and his successors received as a gift at the same time all those immense *imponderabilia* which for the culture of that age were almost inevitably linked with the *urbs:* Roman authority, Roman dominion, Roman order, Roman law, Roman tradition, but also Roman moderation and power of adjustment, Roman prudence, the art of the golden mean. Roman genius brought its gifts to the Rock of Peter. Mistaken as the view would be which would regard the Roman papacy as a mere continuation of the Roman *imperium* and would deny its direct institution by Christ, it is nevertheless certain that it was the Roman spirit that God chose to enlist for the development of the visible part of His Church. A

B   17

glance at the eastern churches makes this beneficent influence of the Roman genius immediately evident. However much the eastern churches recognise in theory the visible lines marked out by Christ for the structure of their ecclesiastical life, above all of the ecclesiastical hierarchy, yet they weaken by their democratic ecclesiastical constitution the power and dignity of that forceful, self-assured authority that flows from the Head, Christ, to His visible organs and members, and furnishes the real guarantee of ecclesiastical discipline, order and law. And because, for that very reason, they recognise the ultimate basis of unity of the Church not in a visible foundation, the Rock of Peter, but in something invisible, in a spiritual communion of love, they lack the power of effective initiative and unity. To fall to pieces, to drop into schism, is in their blood; and their existence can be maintained only artificially by basing their external union upon purely national or ethnic grounds. In place of the one Church of Christ, they became a multiplicity of autocephalous national churches. The fact that western Christianity did not fall to pieces into such a multiplicity, that its horizon was never narrowed to a merely national range of vision, that it saw from the very beginning its visible foundation in the Rock of Peter and in a super-national unity instituted by the will of Christ, and that this supernational unity enabled it to unite the Christian peoples into a single *civitas Dei*, a single Christian family of nations—all this western Christendom owed certainly first and foremost to the decisive words of Christ at Caesarea Philippi, *Tu es Petrus*, and to the working of the Holy Ghost, who preserves His Church from error. But that it was western Christendom that had the ears to hear that decision of Jesus and to listen to the working of the Holy Ghost, that in distinction to the East it grasped these sublime authoritative words in their fullest significance, and despite all resistances carried them into effect with unshakable consistency—that was due to the predestination of the Roman genius to assist in the development of the visible Church, its special vocation, thanks to its inherited talents, its marked sense of authority, power and law, for seizing with clear vision the actual outlines of the ecclesiastical constitution created by Christ, and for preserving them against all excesses of a purely mystical contemplation.

This Greek and Roman weft worked into the God-made warp of early Christendom justifies us in speaking of "western Christianity" in a deeper sense than its merely topographical meaning. But still more are we justified by the third factor that became influential in Christianity, which we may call the Germanic element. To avoid all futile discussions, let us take this term not in its strictly ethnological, but in its historical sense. We mean then by "Germanic" peoples not the teutonic races alone, but all those tribes which were set in motion by the national imgrations, overthrew the old Roman Empire, and set up on its ruins, outside the range of the Graeco-Roman world, though not untouched by it, a peculiar mid-European civilisation of their own—a Germanic Christian civilisation—under teutonic leadership. It is this Germanic Christian civilisation which is the special achievement of the Germanic peoples in regard to Christianity. Their youthful, enterprising vigour grasped the Christian message not only in its intellectual and institutional aspects, but also, and especially, from the point of view of its life-giving inner forces. Christianity became bone of their bone, blood of their blood. When the process was completed, a new synthesis had come into being; by the side of Graeco-Roman Christianity there existed a Germanic Christianity. Its specific nature was conditioned by the specific nature of the Germanic peoples, by the creative activity of their spirituality. Whereas the Christianity of the East and of the churches influenced by the East was mainly passive, and remained passive in its heroic, confident yielding of the soul to the eternal goods of the beyond whose earnest was found in the Christian mysteries, and thus maintained on the whole an eschatological, mystical attitude, the active nature of the Germanic peoples urged them rather to a realisation, if possible, of these goods in the present, in this world. For them the kingdom of God, ultimately to descend from Heaven, casts its radiance even now upon the earth, in the *civitas Dei* uniting all nations, where there are but two swords, that of the Pope and that of the

Emperor. The future heavenly *Pax*, the eternal peace, finds its reflexion even now in that cosmos in which material things are ordered towards spiritual and spiritual towards the divine, terrestrial towards the ecclesiastical, natural towards the supernatural, thought towards faith. The sublime beauty of Heaven, seen and caught by eastern art in its rigid permanence and eternity, is here cast into the mould of the present moment, radiant in terrestrial human beauty. And just as the Germanic peoples in the face of the relation of eternity and time, of hither-worldliness and the beyond, emphasise *this* world and endeavour to grasp the eternal in time, so they also stress in the relation of Divine Grace and human will, of sacrament and works, of *opus operatum* and *opus operantis*, especially the human working, its initiative and its effect. The new life promised by Christ is to them not only, as it is to the eastern mind, a precious gift whose foretaste we enjoy in the Mysteries, but at the same time a permanent task of man, the act of the moment to be accomplished here and now. As for that reason it was only in the Germanic and western soil that Pelagianism and semi-Pelagianism were able to take root, so it was there that all those forms of piety sprang up which lay stress upon personal effort, such as the practices of penance and indulgences and the immense number of private devotional exercises. It was only here that in time a theology developed which gives in the interplay of grace and freedom the leading part to the human will.

From this point of view the system of Molina is a typically western and Germanic product which could not have taken root in eastern Christianity.

The same Germanic tendency towards an activity which strives to transfer the eternal and Divine to the plane of the temporal and terrestrial, is noticeable also in the third relation peculiar to the message of Christ: the relation of faith and knowledge. No sooner had western theology completed the study and inventory of patristic wisdom than the Germanic mind (Germanic in the sense given to that term above) began on its own initiative to review this heritage dialectically and speculatively, to secure its foundations, to clear up its connexions and to deduce further truths from its data: scholasticism arose. Scholasticism is the ambitious attempt of western Christianity to become conscious of itself as far as possible, to render sensible to itself the truths of revelation as held not only by faith but by reason, to transpose the word of God from its sublime transcendence to a sort of immanence in the human mind. The danger of intruding upon the mysteries of God was obvious, and it was not only Abelard who succumbed to it. It was the *princeps scholasticorum*, St. Thomas Aquinas, who finally dispelled it. He succeeded in setting up reason entirely on its own feet and at the same time in giving to faith what properly pertains to it : following his great Swabian teacher, Albertus Magnus, he replaced the Platonic-Augustinian theory of illumination by the doctrine of the *intellectus agens* and the *habitus primorum princi-piorum,* and restricted the supernatural light to the sphere of faith. Only thus could a clear distinction be made between faith and reason, between theology and philosophy; and on the basis of this distinction alone could the mystery of Christian faith be safe-guarded. Only now was the road clear by which thought, established in its own right but conscious of its limitations, could launch out in the unfettered play of its strength upon the gigantic venture, if not of comprehending, at least of embracing the entire field of reality, revelation and nature, God and the world, in a single great *Summa.* Now the light broke in the life of Christendom: not indeed, the noonday light of the immediate vision of God, but at least a dawn that hid even while it revealed.

The peculiar achievement of the Germanic spirit in Christianity consists in having thus applied with immense energy the fundamental truth of the pre-eminent function of the Logos, which had always been present to the Church, to the entire range of natural and supernatural reality without exception. In the last resort it is this rational element and the corresponding resistance to everything illogical and irrational which distinguished western from eastern Christianity. However faithfully eastern theology preserved the rational elements embedded in the trinitarian and christological speculations, it also confined itself, especially after its separation from the western Church, to mere tradition, to the handing

23

on of the wisdom of the Fathers and the great Saints. The Holy Ghost proceeds no longer also from the Logos (*filioque*), but becomes independent. Speculative theology dies or passes over into mysticism. Therewith every dogmatic process is spent and every need of magisterial decisions. The sustenance of the devout Christian is no longer the clear pronouncement of the gospel, the sermon, the catechism, dogmatic theology, but the awe and reverence of mystery. It is his painful joy to see and to affirm the antinomies of his faith in the denials of his negative theology, and to adore in silence the ineffable mystery, the ἄρρητον of Divine Being. Eastern Christianity, far from tending towards the dawn of day, rather takes refuge in the darkness of mystery to wait confidently for the liberating light illuminating the Last Day.

The characteristic influence of the Germanic mind upon Christianity lies thus in the fact that the Germanic peoples conceived it in their youthful energy and optimistic outlook as a present living force in life, with the result that, while devoutly waiting for the completion of time, they were especially susceptible to that other word of Christ: *the kingdom is "in you."* This is the reason why western Christianity has never felt as acutely or as harshly as the eastern mind, the cleft between this world and the world beyond. The sense of this void has been lessened by the strong belief in a Divine immanence. This is a specifically Germanic product; as also in general, Aryan spirituality, as far as one can judge from its writings, shows the unmistakable tendency to gather up God and the world into a single term and to foster, even to exaggerate, the notion of immanence as opposed to the transcendence of God. A characteristic result of this tendency in the sphere of theology is Modernism. It exaggerated the immanence of God into a denial of God as above us. By killing this Modernism, Pius X saved the Christian message from the excesses and exaggerations of the Germanic mind.

If we now cast back our glance over these relations of the genius of Greece, of Rome and of the Germanic peoples to Christianity, we may say that it pleased God to enlist the western mind in a special measure for the message of Christ and to bring it in a special way into its service. The best forces of western Europe are invested in Christianity and they partake therefore to a certain extent of the permanence of the message itself. This relation to Christianity is so intimate and essential that we may say that Christianity is the destiny of the western mind. In serving Christ it serves in the highest sense itself. If it abandons Christ, it falls away from the best part of itself. The question of the future of the western lands is : will they remain faithful to their special vocation for Christianity? will they continue to bear in future centuries the *onus Christi* imposed upon them by this vocation? The vocation to be a χριστοφόρος is the beginning and end of the West.

3

We have now secured the basis for an answer to our second question: What is the attitude of the western mind to Christ now, in our own time?

It is a question of the utmost gravity which here confronts us. Are we not faced with an entirely novel situation? Is not the western mind nowadays not only estranged from Christ, but even hostile to Him? If we should have to answer in the affirmative, the power and majesty of Christ would not thereby be in any way diminished. Even so, he would remain the Master, the King who has the right to command. But our western lands would stand before him, no longer as the disciple who first obeyed the call, but as the accused, as the lazy servant who buried his talent; subject and responsible to Christ, no longer by reason of the greatness and sublimity of their original vocation, but by reason of the greatness and depth of their fall, their sin. A hard, overwhelming duty of restitution, of expiation would weigh on them. Has the West this duty?

i. The roots of our question go back to before the Reformation. Even before Luther and Calvin the western mind had turned against Christ. Not in the sense that Christ had been widely denied in the sphere of personal spirituality; all the same, by the end of the Middle Ages, he had ceased to rule the spirit of the times. It was the great sin of the West even before Luther, that the spirit of the times, the objective forms of the western mind embodied in the state, in economic life, in science and art, were progressively withdrawn from the rule of Christ. It had been the greatest achievement of the Christian West to assert the Kingship of Christ not only for the individual soul, but in the entire range of its economic, cultural and political life, and to create a cosmos in which every form of natural existence culminated in the supernatural life. It was now its greatest misdeed to lay hand itself upon this cosmos, to tear piece after piece from its supernatural context, to profane and to violate it. This process of emancipation by which the West, even before Luther, shook the scientific, economic and political forms of its life loose from their supernatural setting, was a secret but all the more dangerous attempt against Christ, because it necessarily entailed not only the emancipation but also a form of idolisation of natural ends and orders. It was the beginning of a slave-revolt of the western mind against the spirit of Christ.

It is well-known that a whole series of historical factors favoured this process of emancipation and that it was not least ecclesiastical abuses that furthered it. The ecclesiastical-political troubles of the Middle Ages are not least responsible for the fact that the secular sword was gradually withdrawn from the influence of the spiritual, that nations became more and more independent and therewith broke down the real union of the Christian West, and— a far more serious and dangerous development—

that the spiritual basis of this unity also, the intimate union with the Vicar of Christ, the confidence and faith in the guidance of Rome, entered upon an insidious crisis. Such factors were the wars between Popes and Emperors and other rulers, not always conducted in the spirit of the King of Peace, the gross scandals of schisms within the Church, the abuses in the management of papal finances which increased during the exile in Avignon. To this must be added the constantly growing spirit of worldliness since the thirteenth century. Nor was it wholly the fault of profane science that the emancipation of political life was followed by the declaration of independence of scientific and cultural thought from the jurisdiction of Faith; that the distinction between faith and knowledge established by St. Thomas was gradually developed into a hostile opposition between the growing secular disciplines and theology; that finally even philosophy rebelled against its ancillary position to theology and proceeded, for its part, to tyrannise over theology; and that—again a much graver and more dangerous step—the very authority of ecclesiastical teaching suffered immense loss of prestige and confidence. Theology, enticed by the Aristotelian conception of science, had ventured too far on the thin ice of abstract speculation and had lost all contact with actual life. At the very time when the new scientific picture of the world took form and the gaze penetrated into the endless vistas of the cosmos and the endless depths of organic and inorganic life, there was no second St. Thomas to teach us to read the newly-discovered book with the eyes of faith. Theology was wholly unprepared for these new discoveries, and failed catastrophically, although it would have needed but a fundamental return to its own axioms and principles to avert the suspicion of being the born enemy of all serious research. And so it came lamentably to pass that a great part of all the new knowledge was acquired, not in the service of theology as formerly, but without it and even in spite of it.

Thus there were serious failures even *intra muros*. But these failures were not the motive causes of that process of emancipation which began with the fourteenth century, but only factors promoting it. The motive causes of the process lay rather in the peculiarities of the western mind itself and in the excess and exaggeration of the very forces which in the flowering period of western Christianity had furthered its development. It looked as if these forces wished to revenge themselves for having been pressed into the service of the temple. Greek thought and its passion for the $\theta\epsilon\omega\rho\iota\alpha\iota$ which had been so valuable for the rational formulation of the truths of revelation, were gradually exaggerated into the one-sided intellectualism of the later scholasticism; thence it was but a step to the rationalism of the Age of Enlightenment and, thence again, to the autonomy of pure reason. The desire for autonomy all round, the tendency to a self-complacent self-completeness, shy of all authority and hostile to it, awoke then of itself. The political and juridical sense of the Roman, so important a factor in the development of canon and civil law, in the growth of a visible juridically governed Church and in the relations between Papacy and Empire, created of itself in the course of history occasions for so serious a friction between secular and ecclesiastical authorities that the emancipation of the state, of society and economic life appeared as a natural consequence. And the very urge of the Germanic mind towards productive activity and the realisation of its ideals, however helpful towards the actualisation and vivid consciousness of the Christian truths and values, gave itself over with equal energy to the empirical sciences, the exploration of nature and its forces, and prepared thereby a development which was bound to lead to the autonomy of technical and industrial life, of labour and capital. Indeed, the very fact that these specific forces of the West yielded to such excesses, and progressively destroyed the essential order of things and their adjustment to their only supernatural end, was in the last resort the result of a religious, ethical failure: the point where the Fall from God begins, secret intellectual pride and megalomania and blind worldly indulgence. That was sin. It was in practice the declaration: *Non serviam*— for the moment often, it is true, below the threshold of consciousness, but later clearly grasped and asserted with emphasis and insistence. The more unmistakably this new anti-christian attitude of mind developed, the more rapidly proceeded the process of secularisation. Almost overnight whole ranges of human civilisation arose, profaned and separated from the jurisdiction of Christ. They had lost their inner nobility, their relation to the Logos, and therewith their Christian soul, their supernatural life and their intimate unity of existence with and for each other. Inevitably, these sub-Christian, even non-Christian, products of culture isolated themselves from each other, combated each other, became idolised as ends in themselves, and ended by tyrannising over mankind like a Moloch. We are nowadays in the middle of this phase of development. *Numeri sumus*: we human beings are henceforth but ciphers before those autocratic, self-complacent, soulless things which we call State, Political Economy, Industry, Science. By setting them free from the jurisdiction of Christ, by making into an absolute end what is merely the part of a whole, and useful only as a part, the western mind has itself become the slave of these new absolute entities. This new age of impersonal ciphers, of a soulless mechanism, of an equality which hates qualitative differences and fanatically levels every internal order of rank, of undifferentiated masses, has been the fruit of that first great sin when the western mind, blinded by intellectual pride, megalomania and worldly self-complacency, set about to withdraw the kingdom of the spirit from the Kingship of Christ, and to secularise it.

ii. The second great sin of the West goes deeper. It is directed not only against the Kingship of Christ upon earth, but against Christ himself, against his Divine Person. As the western mind has laboured like no other to contribute to the outward and inner formation of Christendom, so, like no other, it has been guilty of the destruction of the Christian Faith and of the image of Christ. In the morning of its youth it shouted enthusiastically "Osanna to the Son of David!": as the day declined, the cry was heard *"Crucifige!"*

The first step towards the defection from Christ was taken by the Reformers. However much Luther and Calvin may subjectively have been convinced that it was their task to protect the cause of Christ against the antichrist, their attack upon Rome, viewed objectively, was an attempt upon Christ himself. By opposing a new credo to the old, by setting up altar against altar, church against church, they tore Christendom not in two, but in hundreds and thousands of pieces. Man emancipating himself not only in politics and economics but also in religion from the Church of Christ, claimed autonomy for himself. The victorious word of the one Truth, grace leading all men to salvation, lost its old ring for those outside. For the inner oppositions did not merely touch the surface; they penetrated to the very marrow. The old question of Pilate re-emerged: "What is truth?" This inner disruption of the community of the faithful is the festering wound in the

32

Body of Christ. And as long as this wound is not healed from the inside, as long as western Christendom presents the great scandal of hostile disunion and opposition, it not only is utterly deprived of its recruiting powers, but cannot drain the swamps from which the poisonous weeds of scepticism and unbelief shoot up again and again. To call in doubt the one papal Church was bound to lead to calling in doubt Christ himself. The more, in the course of controversies between Catholics and Protestants, the idea gained ground on both sides that the alleged Catholic errors are to be found at least as early as in St. Paul, nay even in the teaching of the so-called "synoptic Jesus," the nearer was bound to come the time, when non-Catholics believed that Jesus himself could only be regarded as a historically conditioned phenomenon, tinged with the errors of his time, and no longer simply as a Divine super-temporal being.

It is the sad glory of a large part of that theology which proudly considers itself as the heir of Luther and Calvin to have been engaged for decades in this business of a radical destruction of the image of Christ, and to have found an essential part of its task in killing Christ and burying his body. This is the extreme limit which so far the western mind has reached in its emancipation from Christ, the point where this mind is mobilised against Christ himself and sets out for Golgotha so that Christ may die afresh.

A glance at the research into the life of Christ proves that this is no exaggeration. The history of these researches shows two things. First, the fact that the denial of the Divinity of Christ is based by no means on the result of scientific inquiry and the careful and comprehensive examination of sources, but on unbelief as a principle. It is not the product of unbiassed knowledge, but of the depths of demoniacal opposition. Wherever we look among the so-called "liberal" or "critical" christologies, we find at the outset of their enquiries, as their starting-point, even as their decisive principle, that dogma of unbelief which Renan expressed in the words: *Il n'y a pas de surnaturel*. Modern critical theology means the same thing when it states as the basis for its appreciation of the life of Jesus the law of "analogy" with what happens before our very eyes, and that of "correlation," i.e. of the conditional and mutual interdependence of all historical matters. For, since the appearance of Christ as a direct personal entry of God into this spatial and temporal world necessarily transcends and annihilates all analogies and conditions of experience, the demand for analogy and correlation in the working of Christ amounts to nothing less than a tacit denial, antecedent to and prejudging all serious investigation of the supernatural character of our Lord's appearance. Even before the witnesses have been heard, the claim of Jesus to divinity is rejected. Starting from this basis, this "critical" theology can have no other task than to prove Christ and His work to have been but a great deception or self-illusion and to show in detail how most probably this illusion came about and how the Jesus of history became the Christ of faith. The entire formulation of the problem of this critical christology, its analysis of sources, its argumentation, are dominated by this negative, *a priori* unbelief. Its whole scientific apparatus rests on the *credo* of that demon who will not have it that God is God, a super-personal, transcendent, living God who reveals himself with sovereign freedom and omnipotence above and beyond all experiential data, even to having given his own Son.

Connected with this is the second peculiarity of modern christologies, their close dependence upon the spirit of the times, especially on contemporary philosophy: the old saying, *philosophia est ancilla theologiae*, has now been reversed: nothing could be more natural, for this philosophy bears a close resemblance to this theology: it, too, narrowed the human spirit down to the world of phenomena and blocked every vista towards the world of metaphysical truth and the foundations and perspectives beyond experiential being. Since it had extinguished the *lumen fidei*, with inevitable and deplorable necessity it also dimmed the power of transcendental illumination of the *lumen rationis*. In the greater part of the western intellectual woild it killed consequently the capacity for apprehending the supersensuous, not to speak of the supernatural. The intellectual world of the West

35

entered therewith upon a period of an artificial blinding and blindness. People lost the gift of seeing transcendental facts; and the critical christology by surrendering wholesale to this artificially blinded philosophy, borrowed from it its formulæ and schematic constructions in order to dress up its labours of anti-christian destruction in philosophical garb with all the attractions of modern intellectuality. In its hands not only was Christ deprived of His divinity, but even His humanity was completely secularised and conceived in terms of relativity. He might wear the gown of an enlightened philosopher, or again the cap of a Jacobin. Sometimes it was the conceptions of Kant and Hegel, sometimes those of anthropology or even of the psycho-analysis of Freud that served as the mould into which the Person and work of Christ were forced. *Ecce homo*. Naked, Christ the Lord stands tied to the pillar and is scourged and attired in the mantle of derision. Need we wonder, if as a symptom of the contemporary spirit we find whole masses lapsing from Christ? For instance, the "Association for Freethinking and Cremation," founded in 1927, which is pledged to class-war and forbids all religion, counted in the very year of its foundation more than five hundred thousand members. Antichrist is at work as never before. He is beginning to create entire states on the principle of a hatred of Christ. That is the novel and terrible thing. Nothing has ever happened before in the history of western Christianity like this organised mass-defection from Christ. It is the re-enactment on an immense scale of that scene of Capharnaum, when the Master turned to His disciples with the question: "Will you also go away?"

4

More and more the western mind is drifting away from Christ. No doubt even during the flourishing periods of the Christian West there were times of stagnation and even decay. But the general spiritual life was nevertheless markedly Christian. The development moved upwards, Christwards. Even today, it is true, there exist many homes of vigorous faith, many faithful communities of disciples. But the face of the West is nowadays non-Christian, in parts even anti-Christian. The development leads downwards, away from Christ. And inasmuch as Christ, and He alone, is our life, *the* Life, this flight from Christ of the present day is a flight from life, into death: it means destruction.

Are we then to say that Spengler was after all right when he prophesied the decline of the West? He would have been right, if he had not left out of his account two factors which in his naturalistic-morphological treatment of the question were completely neglected, but are precisely the decisive factors, namely God and the soul; in other words, the freedom, spontaneity and impredictability of Divine Provi-

37

dence, and the freedom of the human will. Our future is created not merely by blind natural forces. God has the direction of affairs in His hands even to-day; and now as before the human will is free to follow the call of God and to choose good instead of evil.

Who could venture to say whether or not a Christian revival of the West is part of the free predestination of Divine Providence? We can only assert that the West, despite its sins, is even to-day endowed with certain privileges, certain advantages, certain external "graces" which justify us in thinking that God's call still goes out to it. The Rock of Peter still stands unshaken on the banks of the Tiber. In face of all the disunion and disruption of nations and peoples, and of the break-up of human society, it is still the centre where all the restless turmoil of our modern developments can find its way back to unity. In the midst of our western civilisation there is still an authority, older than all the states, firmer than all the thrones, more powerful than all dictatorships, more sacred than the law of nations. All these, the states, the thrones, the dictatorships and the law of nations are but things of yesterday, the products of time. But this authority in our midst lives by the eternal will of Christ, spirit of his spirit, power of his power. It will for ever proclaim this authority of Christ, for ever be ready as our guide, in order to help us to find our way out of chaos. And on this Rock rests the western Church. Her organisation is still unimpaired; her doctrine still pure; it still receives the homage of obedience of an army of faithful bishops and priests and of a numberless multitude of the faithful, devoted, prepared for sacrifice. There are still tabernacles in the West and men who pray before them. The Body of Christ still finds living members in whom He fulfils himself day by day and who do not bend the knee before Baal. Thus the West is still the privileged place of Divine blessings, where the grace of Christ has not remained without witness.

We may therefore feel with confidence that God will allow the spirit of the West to come to life again—provided that the human will freely follows the call of His grace. But will it? Will it seek the road back to Christ?

We saw how deeply it had involved itself in guilt, how more and more consciously, insistently and com-prehensively its will withdrew from its supernatural purpose, and all its endeavours were set upon a progressive idolisation of natural ends, of second and third-rate values, and how, finally, it penetrated into the Holy of Holies and began to deride Christ Himself. We noted further that it was the excesses of those very forces which once upon a time had been called to the service of the Church, that bore the main guilt for this growing detachment from Christ. They seduced the western mind to the most arid intellectualism, to a self-complacent independence and at the same time to materialism in things of the mind, a blind indulgence of worldliness in everything. It all meant a progressive aberration into the vulgar world of natural ends and a more and more conscious abandonment of the supernatural.

If ever western spirituality is to be restored all along the line to a Christian sense, this can only be achieved by retracing its steps along this false road. "*Retournez à la nature*," Rousseau once exclaimed: now the call goes out to the West: "Back to the supernatural." There, where God is, lie the springs of our strength, of our new order, of our creative youth. Kindliness and love, humility and purity, are to be found where the Child of Bethlehem is; nobility and devotion where the Crucified is. Only there shall we find our peace and our rest, where the words of the risen Christ are heard: *Pax vobiscum*. But we can reach back to the supernatural only by a most determined change of heart, a μετάνοια. The western mind will have to become quite small again, in order to make room for the supernatural. It must turn again, from the surface of its being where the intellect plays its calculating game with the things of this world, to its innermost being where the things of this world are silent and God speaks. Only in the depths of such a merciless return to itself, when its whole being is pressed back into one point and the cold, clear light of eternal things plays upon it, will it be able to realise the enormity of its questionable, dishonest and godless doings. Only such conscious vision is capable of seeing the crucified Christ; only hearts shaken to their depths can find the supernatural; only the fully contrite man is on the right road to God.

This applies not only to those who are outside the fold. It applies equally to us, practising Catholics, even to us especially. There are, indeed, few truths which the Church impresses upon our conscience with the same emphasis and ruthlessness as that of our supernatural vocation and of our duty to do penance. But the spirit of the West all the same continously colours the manner in which we listen to the message of the Church and dims the purity, austerity and vigour of our supernatural life.

We can observe the influence of western *intellectualism* in the atrophy which infects the spiritual attitude of so many Catholics. Their faith often is reduced to a purely intellectual and therefore shallow awareness of the teaching of the Church and to a mere assent of the mind, pronounced as easily as our mind assents to the things of this world. And yet every *credo*, if said in the spirit of the Church, ought to be an act of completest dedication of the entire man to God, the Person of persons, a determined surrender to the Absolute of Divine Truth and truthfulness; an assent springing from the great and ineffable distress of our finite nature and our sin, vibrating with the silent, secret struggles of our soul to find itself and its God; an assent called forth by the touch of eternal Love, an assent of the Holy Ghost, a first flash of the supernatural reality of our soul, *donum Dei*, a Mystery. This *credo* alone, is the foundation and root of our justification. It lives not on the surface of our being, in our intellect only; nor does it harden into a mere cult of sacred words and formulæ, for there is too much reverence and humility, too much struggle and sorrow in it for it ever to degenerate into a pharisaical zealotry. It is rather the germinating life in the Holy Ghost, a life that knows no rest and grows and grows until that love has taken form in it without which even the faith that moves mountains would be as nothing (I *Cor.* xiii, 2). We need but ask ourselves whether this faith is in us and in all who call themselves the Catholic faithful, to observe to our shame and horror how crudely it has become with many an affair of external form, how deeply the western intellectualism has infected and corroded our fundamental religious attitude.

No less are we threatened by the western propensity to self-complacent autonomy. It awakens in our spiritual life only too easily the defiance of a proud self-determination, a distrust of, and mania to criticise, ecclesiastical authority. The faithful infected with it cease to live in and with the Church, as flesh of her flesh; they live alongside her, in a sphere of existence which they have carefully marked off from the Church. They see the Church merely as an object, at the best as an institution of truth and grace. They fail to see her at the same time as subject, as the fountain and foundation of their own spiritual personality and as that sacred and sublime community in which Christ as the Head is linked with His members in a real supernatural union. They fail to see her, or see her but dimly, as the Body of Christ. Their attitude therefore lacks that really creative humility, that fertile openmindedness and vigorous wholeness and joy which is the fruit springing naturally from the sense of this supernatural community-life.

In its practical aspect the Germanic spirit of this self-centred autonomy assumes easily that form of individual piety against which Abbot Ildefons Herwegen has already raised his warning voice. The individual isolates himself, as much as he can, from the community of the mystical Christ, of the One Bread. "His" prayer, "his" confession, "his" mass, "his" communion, "his" other devotions—they belong, it is true, from the objectively dogmatic point of view, to the entire Christ and live with the breath of the sacred Communion; but he, in his prayers, is often no longer conscious of that. He prays *solus cum solo*, like an isolated being, so to speak "privately." Yet such prayer runs counter to the fundamental law of the Body of Christ and the life of its members with and for one another. Thus dispersing, we do our best to shatter the power for unity immanent in the Body of Christ and transcending all nations and civilisations, in all its concentrated fullness, into a thousand fragments. We deprive ourselves through our own fault of the strongest guarantee of our inner victorious superiority. If it is indeed Collectivism which in the rhythm of spiritual movements will replace in the not far distant

43

future the western individualism, then there is more
need than ever for us to find our way back to this
essential fundamentally Christian attitude irrespec-
tive of temporary conditions, and to oppose to the
approaching materialistic cosmopolitanism of social-
ists and communists the Body of Christ, that organism
which has been tried in millions of Christian consciences even to the verge of blood, has stood the test
of centuries and forms the unbreakable supernatural
union of "the many in the One Bread."

It is hardly necessary to point out how this tendency, taken over by our piety from the spirit of the
West, towards a theoretical and practical individualism, is apt to turn only too easily into a bare-
faced egoism, not only in social and economic
matters, but also in religion. It leads not infre-
quently to a selfish misuse of the supernatural
means of grace, of the Church and her sacraments,
to egoistical exploitation and idolisation of them.
Instead of piercing to the last, fruitful depths of the
sacraments of the Church, where humility and
reverence, purity and love, make up the image of
the *homo sanctus*, interest in religion and Church does
not go beyond the external legitimate use of the
Church's means of grace. They are turned into other
forms of perversely refined egoism, a demand for
outward importance, authority or power, a sensuous
transport of sentiment, or—the most sublime but
therefore most dangerous form of idolisation—the
demand for an unerring, unconditional, absolute

assurance of ultimate salvation. What is lacking in this piety is the seriousness of the Last Things, the fear of the coming Judgment, a fear which even the most pious Christian cannot escape, and the constant struggling and straining after the Last End. We act as if the decision had already been made, as if the magnificence, power and beatitude of the Resurrection were our assured portion already in this life. Thus we meet the conceited, blasé Catholic, or the sentimental pietist, or the vehement, narrow-fronted Pharisee, proud of his descent from Abraham. Faith degenerates into making debating-points, now and then into fanaticism that kills love; piety grows into a mere observance of the law and a merely external activity; the Church becomes a mere party object. Nothing disfigures the sublime image of piety and the sacredness of our supernatural vocation so intolerably, nothing impedes so uncannily the appeal of Holy Church, as this misuse of holy things. No wonder that our Lord has condemned nothing so severely as this (*Mt.* xxiii).

Like intellectualism and its self-satisfied pride, the worldliness of the western mind is not unknown in contemporary Catholicism. It is so deeply embedded in our souls that ordinarily we are quite unconscious of it. Only when the *Deus crucifixus* is preached to us and we are reminded of our duty to bear the cross and to deny ourselves, do we become for a flash aware of the immense chasm which yawns between the kingdom of God and the world, and we find ourselves

45

balancing upon that point where a decision has to be taken. This decision is taken, of course, not in external forms. For the kingdom of God, which alone is in question, is not "here and there" (*Lk*. xvii, 21); it is something super-terrestrial, supernatural, Divine. So it may well be that someone in the midst of a worldly civilisation, perhaps even on its very summit, is yet searching after and finding the heavenly pearl in the depths of his soul. This decision, this cleavage does not cut along visibly perceptible lines across different civilisations; it does not divide a so-called "Christian" civilisation from others; it does not even outline the Church: it cuts through the consciences alone. Even medieval man, however much he belonged to a uniform civilisation and the only Church, was not spared the alternatives of this decision, this inner break. Yet, however inward an affair this decision is, its range of action is not limited to the heart of our personality or to our religious and moral reformation, but irradiates inevitably our surrounding world, our civilisation, our economic life. Even if these do not change in their structure, yet the manner changes in which we, the late comers, regard them, estimate them and use them. For that reason the paradox of the "kingdom of Heaven," its being something quite different, must, after all, somehow become visible in our economic and cultural make-up—at least it ought to be so visible. It ought for those outside, the non-Christians, somehow to be evident that we are not, like the children of the world, gathering the riches of the earth where they are devoured by rust and moths and anxiously worrying and asking "What shall we eat, what shall we drink; wherewith shall we clothe ourselves?"; that we are not resisting evil, but if someone strikes us on the right cheek, we offer him also the left. Always the new gospel and the Kingdom of Heaven in us will insist upon taking its own peculiar form, the poor Crib and the dishonour of the Cross.

In the light of all this, we see how much we are all infected by the worldliness of the West. *Nostra culpa, nostra maxima culpa*! It has been not the least fault of our worldliness that the poor and oppressed have lost confidence in us and think the Church is but an instrument of the wealthy. This worldliness robbed us of that simplicity of conduct, that poverty of spirit and brotherliness of mind which alone could have won and held the confidence of the disinherited of this world. Because we have not taken the supernatural and its demands sufficiently seriously, we lapse widely into open or veiled snobbery and pride of education and possessions. "The name of God was derided by us among the heathen" (*Rom.* ii, 24). So it happened that we estranged from us precisely those who out "on the crossroads and streets" are called more than all others "to fill the wedding hall" (*Mt.* xii, 9, 10). Even to-day our Lord likes to dwell nowhere better than among the taxgatherers and sinners, even to-day his beatitudes are addressed not to those who are rich and well fed, but to those who are suffering and persecuted. To-day when

47

poverty stalks the streets and the idol of mammon disinherits millions and keeps them in permanent servitude, pitilessly destroying the happiness of family life and with unparalleled levity inflaming class-hatred—even to-day there is still room and a fertile field for the Saviour's work to be done by the Church. But it cannot be done merely by beautiful sermons. Even the great social organisations are no longer sufficient, not even the devoted labours of charitable societies. The only remedy is a new life in the Holy Ghost, a return of all of us to the paradox of the supernatural, a determined assent to the poor, crucified Jesus. That is the road to the re-birth of the West; there is no other way. Μετανοείτε.

The path to reform is then clear. But, indeed, when describing this path, our heart fears and we should like to exclaim with the Apostle: "Lord, who then can be saved?" It is quite evident to us that we, the West, will not of our own accord set foot upon this path leading to the poor, crucified Jesus. But are not all things possible with God (*Mk*. x, 27)? Perhaps the Lord Christ will call again from His Church apostles and saints who, attired in the strength from on high, will bring a new spring into His Church. Perhaps He will give us a second St. Francis, a saint with a burning heart, who will seek and love poverty in human life in the brutal nakedness of its reality, in the many forms of its oppressiveness, narrowness and savagery; who will set out daily with his brethren to bear himself side by side with his children the hard yoke of dull factory-work, to share with them their poor food and their bare lodgings; who ultimately will pray with them and lead them in to the wedding-feast. Or perhaps that God will come to us in storm and tempest and we shall have to descend again into the catacombs in order to find Christ. I cannot tell, but this much I know: whether God's grace renews us in the whispering of the breeze or the roar of the storm, it will renew us only by making us small again.

What are we to do, oh, my brothers, my sisters? We are the collaborators of Christ, Christ's soldiers in the battle against anti-Christ. Perhaps Christ needs but three hundred men to overthrow the Amalekites. Perhaps only a dozen men of the people would suffice Him as they sufficed once before. But He needs their hearts, their blood. If we all had dared to make the great break-through from externals to the inner being, from the world to God, from our sensuous *ego* to the new man in Christ; if we all had passed through the great contrition and the fear of a serious penance in which earthly things lose their glamour and supernatural things flame as the new reality; if we all loved God with all our hearts, and if through Christ we loved our brethren; if we learnt this at the table of the Lord and understood that those who share with us in the Body of the Lord become our nearest relatives, one single *communio sanctorum*; if in the strength of this new life and this new love we could see also our western lands with new eyes, not only their faults but their virtues also, their desire for truth, their strong self-reliance, their open-mindedness; if we developed these virtues also in ourselves and stood up to the children of the world and, like them but with our new hearts, explored the wonders of nature and discovered the secrets of science, eager to find the traces of God in nature and to imitate his wisdom constructively; if we loved our Church, this vision of the supernatural upon earth, as a child loves its mother, not in external obedience but with the devotion of our hearts because our conscience demands nothing less; if, faithful to this conscience, we all shared the sense of responsibility for whatever happens in the Church and through her; if we lived and suffered and fought together with her, not like the Sons of Thunder who called down the fire from heaven upon the faithless cities, but zealous in that quiet steady love even unto death which our Divine Master has shown us; if, in doing so, we were not servile in mind but upright and honest and only sought what is of God; if ever such a new type of man could be in Christ, a *tertium genus*, a new generation, born of the Blood of Christ and consecrated by the Holy Ghost—then God might grant through his mercy that our little lives should kindle a new life in the West and that we all might be spared the threatening visitation of the future.

"When he drew near, seeing the city, he wept over it saying: If thou also hadst known, and that in this thy day, the things that are to thy peace . . . " (*Lk.* xix, 41, 42).   We are that Jerusalem to which Jesus draws near and which he sees before him—we people of the West.   Lord Jesus, grant that we may all know the things that are to our peace!

LOVE AND BELIEF

LOVE AND BELIEF

Once upon a time—so the Babylonic Talmud runs—a pagan came to the Rabbi Shammai and said: "I am willing to become a Jew, if you can explain to me the entire Jewish law in the time during which I can stand on one leg." Shammai dismissed him. He thereupon went to the Rabbi Hillel and made the same request to him. Hillel at once answered: "Do not do to your neighbour whatever you would hate to have done to you. That is the entire law. Everything else is but the commentary to it. Go and learn to do that."

The New Testament tells of a similar incident. A scribe came to Jesus and asked him: "Master which is the great commandment in the law?" Jesus said to him: "Thou shall love the Lord thy God with thy whole heart, and with thy whole soul, and with thy whole mind. This is the greatest and the first commandment. And the second is like to this: Thou shalt love thy neighbour as thyself. On these two commandments dependeth the whole law and the prophets" (*Mt.* xxii, 36, *sqq*). Jesus thus mentions two commandments, not only one, and he places first the commandment of the love of God; but He too observes that the entire law is comprised in these commandments to love. And in the Sermon on the

53

Mount He even reduces the whole law, like Hillel, to love of one's neighbour: "All things therefore whatsoever you would that men should do to you, do you also to them. For this is the law and the prophets" (*Mt.* vii, 12; *Lk.* vi, 31). This formulation differs from that of Hillel only by the fact that Jesus states the essence of the law not negatively, but positively. The law is fulfilled not merely by not doing evil to one's neighbour, but by doing to him all the good that one would like to see done to oneself. Determined devotion to others, active service to our brother, brotherly love: that is the essence which matters above all. Our Lord emphasises with great solemnity that it is in this faithful, devoted love to our brothers that we are to see the new, specific feature of his message: "A new commandment I give unto you: That you love one another, as I have loved you, that you also love one another. By this shall all men know that you are my disciples, if you have love for one another" (*Jn.* xiii, 34-5).

The essence of Christianity is therefore exhaustively expressed by the word "love." Nor have the disciples of Jesus understood their Master otherwise than in this sense. "Follow after charity," demands St. Paul (1 *Cor.* xiv, 1); "Charity is the bond of perfection" (*Col.* iii, 14); "by charity of the spirit serve one another, for"—and here St. Paul repeats the words of Jesus—"all the law is fulfilled in one word: Thou shalt love thy neighbour as thyself" (*Gal.* v, 13-4). St. James calls the commandment to love "the royal law" (*Jas*. ii, 8). St. Peter says that "charity covereth a multitude of sins" (1 *Pet*. iv, 8). And St. John, the subtle, favourite disciple of our Lord, goes deeper and points out the metaphysical basis of the essence of love, when he writes, (1 *Jn*. iv, 7, 8): "Dearly beloved, let us love one another: for charity is of God. And everyone that loveth is born of God and knoweth God. He that loveth not knoweth not God: for God is charity."

The disciples of the Apostles and the subsequent centuries took over this gospel of love from the Apostles. The oldest non-biblical document that we know, the *Didache*, which represents in its teaching of the "two ways" a sort of primitive Christian catechism, opens with these words: "The way to life is this: first, thou shalt love God who has created thee; secondly: thou shalt love thy neighbour as thyself. But whatsoever thou wilt not that be done to thee, do not thou also to thy neighbour" (1, 2). The same is said by Clement of Rome, by Ignatius of Antioch, by Polycarp and all the other Fathers. St. Augustine, the saintly bishop with the glowing heart, erects his entire theological system on the basis of charity. Illuminated by it, he penetrates into the depth of the Triune God and finally ventures upon the bold saying: *Ama et fac quidquid vis*—"Act in charity and you can do whatsoever you will."

If then Christianity is in essence love, is not Christianity something incredibly simple and at the same time marvellously luminous, something which must

55

win all hearts by nothing more than its sheer inner beauty. Why then the hard, strict duty of faith? Why the rigid dogmas, the wearying symbols of Councils of the Church? Why all that immense apparatus of the Church: Pope, bishops, priests? Why this vast, complicated ecclesiastical administration and the *Codex Juris Canonici*? Is not the Gospel, this joyous, simple, luminous message of love, made, *pro tanto*, wearisome and oppressive? Is it not an unbearable burden that is laid thereby upon man? If it is true that love constitutes the essence of Christianity, is it not also true that everything outside this sphere of love, all the external ecclesiastical trappings, all outward dogmatic faith, is something merely peripheral, secondary, even something that leads, experience shows, away from the essence of Christianity, something that hinders, even kills love? Is it not just because of the dogmas that love has suffered the fiercest injuries, that it has been drowned in floods of blood and burnt at the stake? Is it not again to-day still the rigidity, the dogmatism, the external Church that divides men and nations in their most intimate feelings and makes the gospel of Christian love an object of derision? Ought we not really with Tolstoy and Dostoevsky to condemn and curse the churches and all ecclesiastical creations as anti-Christian, even satanic products, as the creations of the spirit of this world in which there still lives the sinister figure of the grand inquisitor who in the name of faith drags love to the scaffold?

These are serious and difficult questions. They demand an answer. Is it really the case that faith kills love? Or at least that faith hinders and impedes its pure working? What is the relation between faith and love?

It is certainly true: Love is the essence of Christianity. Faith without love is but a "dead faith." Such faith even the devils have (*Jas.* ii, 18, 19). "If I should have all faith, so that I could remove mountains, and have not charity, I am nothing" (*I Cor.* xiii, 2). But is it not strange that these same men who as with burning tongues praise charity, will not desist from their faith? With the same emphasis with which they exhort to love, they demand faith. The same sacred lips that announced to us the new commandment of His love, uttered those threatening words: "He that believeth not shall be condemned" (*Mk.* xvi, 16; *cf. Jn.* iii, 36). The same St. John who said that charity was born of God, said also: "Whosoever believeth that Jesus is Christ is born of God" (*I Jn.* v, 1). And however enthusiastically St. Paul sings the high canticle of love, much more often, much more gravely and insistently he speaks of faith and its hidden wonders. It is the high triumph of the Christian that "by grace he is saved through faith" (*Eph.* ii, 8). And the later ages learnt from the Apostles. So much was faith at all times recognised as the very foundation of Christianity that the Christians were simply called the "faithful" (*fideles*).

So there is after all a connexion between faith and love! Is it perhaps that only he can really love who believes? In that case faith would be the spring of real love, and there would be no love where there is no faith? In other words: faith and love, should we say, stand in a sort of causal relation to each other?

In order to clear up these questions, we must first be clear what Christ and His disciples mean when they speak of love. There is hardly a word that is so handled, so worn, as the word "love." But for Jesus it was wholly unambiguous. When He spoke of love, He was not referring to sentimental moods which come to-day and go to-morrow, aim only at the satisfaction of a personal, lower or higher appetite and are in the last resort merely relevant and related to the *ego*. In its formal aspect love is for Him an act of the will; as regards its content it is selfless service rendered to the "neighbour." And the "neighbour" means he who here and now is nearest to me, nearer than father and mother, not only he who is a relative or a friend, but every human being who is in need, be he Samaritan or pagan or Jew. The love of the neighbour, according to Jesus, passes beyond all personal, social, national and religious divisions. It seeks man *"per se,"* precisely among the ruins of sin and want. His care, His labour and troubles, His miracles and his vigils are devoted to this man. "He went about doing good" (*Acts* x, 38). In this service rendered to the neighbour there is no room for prudent reserve, not even towards the prostitute, no careful weighing

58

and hesitation, but sheer determined venture and high-souled action. "If a man ask thee to go with him a mile, go thou two with him." This devotion is so limitless, so unconditional, so wholly a determination of the will, that it does not recoil before the hardest task, even before the sacrifice of our own life. "I have not come to be served, but to serve and to give my life for many." Jesus has confirmed this commandment of love on the cross.

Jesus then means by love the staking of our entire personality on behalf of our brother in need, be he who he may: service to our fellow-man even to the limit of self-sacrifice. "Greater love has no man but that he should give his life for his friends."

As we see, Jesus places before us an ideal of love, overflowing with energy, illuminated by devotion, saturated with the blood of sacrifice. Never before had any prophet set up before mankind or lived an ideal of love with such impressiveness and energy, of such delicacy and affection, so embracing and exhaustive as Jesus, the bringer of this new love. It is only through him that mankind discovered what true love means.

But why does Jesus insist upon so limitless, so severe and even cruel a love, a love even to death? It is nothing less than this question which brings us to the very heart of the message of love of Jesus. Is it the charm of a high-minded humanity that captivated Him? Does He see in man, like Auguste Comte, an "*être suprême*," the absolute, ultimate value, to whom everything has to be sacrificed? Nothing could be more mistaken. Jesus was no philanthropist with an enthusiasm for the cult of the merely human. He was too profound and too whole to feel any enthusiasm for man. He perceived but too clearly beneath the varnish of the purely human the all-too-human sides of him. If we look closer, we might even detect in His attitude to man something like a restrained disgust. Does He not call even Peter—one of his most intimate disciples, who has just solemnly acclaimed Him as Messias—a "satan"? And he uses the expression with an eye to all His disciples who, he knew, shared Peter's opinion (*Mk*. viii, 33). He had selected as His disciples plain, seemingly straight, unwarped men, the best He could find. Yet He knew that what linked them to His person was an egoistical motive, the hope for the twelve thrones of Israel. He knew moreover that one of the plain simple people who at the moment were so affectionately attached to Him would deny Him in the hour of His need, and another would betray Him, and all of them would run away.

No, no—it was not the merit of humanity that Jesus loved man. "*Omnis homo mendax*"—he knew that as well as, he knew that better than, anyone. How petty, how insignificant were the men of the world that surrounded Him. Narrow-minded, blockheaded, ambitious pharisees, frivolous, cynical Sadducees, the dissolute, credulous people, swayed by every mood of the moment—those were the types of men, certainly no better, but also certainly no worse than others over in Rome or down in Alexandria. Such men are not the ultimate, highest value whom one loves and sacrifices one's life for. If this sort of humanity were the only consideration, then love would be sheer delusion and self-deception. In that case, we ought to shake the dust from our feet and preach a quite different gospel: the gospel of our own *ego*, the gospel of "the Only One and His All." [1]

But then why did Jesus all the same love these men even to the sacrifice of Himself, and why does he demand from His disciples this same love?

It is just where he speaks of the hardest, most difficult love, that for our enemies, that the point becomes clearest: "Pray for them that persecute and calumniate you: that you may be the children of your Father who is in heaven, who maketh his sun to rise upon the good and the bad and raineth upon the just and the unjust. . . Be you therefore perfect as also your heavenly Father is perfect" (*Mt.* v, 44, *sqq.*). So Jesus finds the determining motive of his love for men not in men, but in God. The human value is not the ultimate, but only the penultimate value; the last, the highest value is God the Father. He alone is the cause and the measure of all things, cause and measure of all valuations, cause and measure of all love. Because this Father loves men—no matter whether they

[1] *"Der Einzige und sein Eigentum"*: this is the title of the work of the noted solipsist Max Stirner, published 1844, which became notorious later during the period of enthusiasm for Nietzsche (Translator's note).

are good or bad—and because we prove ourselves
His children precisely by showing that same love, are
we to love men. My relation to men has therefore its
ultimate roots in a transcendental fact, namely in
that fundamental relation of love in which God
includes men, all men. Man is a mystery. He is the
culmination-point of an eternal love which issues
from God; a point in the actuality of the world where,
as nowhere else, the love of God burns. That is the
reason why man is worth loving: not by reason of
what he is in himself or for himself, but by reason of
what he is for God; or in the language of theology:
not for a natural but for a supernatural reason. I
shall never reach man by starting from the earth;
I must first reach to heaven to find man through
God. The floodstream of the love of man passes
through the heart of God. I must first have God,
before I can have man. God is the way to man.

Jesus states therewith a fact which is an essential
feature of love. We shall realise this fact as soon as we
recall once more what "Christian love" is meant to
signify. As was said before, its characteristic trait is
its complete detachment from all personal, social and
national considerations, its selflessness, and, connected therewith, its active tension, its readiness for
sacrifice. Wherever this characteristic is lacking,
we find merely the bastard of this true love, an
apocryphal distortion of it. What we human beings
mean when we speak of real love is fulfilled only in
such a love of selflessness and energy. Wherever

love is egocentric and therefore selfish, it has lost its peculiar nuance, the sweetness of its scent, its special savour. When it finds its satisfaction in mere wishing without proceeding to self-sacrificing action, it is merely stuffy and sentimental, a mere wave of a mood, a flower without fruit, which dies even before being put forth.

What now is the answer to the question: is such a selfless, active love, ready thus to realise itself in action, intelligible from the point of view of the actual world? Has it even any sense? If I consider actuality simply in itself, isolated I mean from its supporting, metaphysical basis, detached from God, then there cannot, nay there ought not to be any higher value than my own ego. It is only by reason of my own self that I can posit or affirm extra-personal values. For they are values only so far as I feel them to be values, because of their egocentricity. It may be that outside myself there are still higher values than I; it may be that this or that is better, more perfect than I—but all that is mere supposition, never a certitude, and the fact remains in any case that I am the most certain fact for myself, that my self is my world, my domain, and that everything else can exist for me only inasmuch as it adjusts itself to my world and domain. I alone am my own king and master, my only and highest value, my all.

Seen from this purely logical standpoint, all unselfish, disinterested love is foolishness. For it would be a venture, a leap in the dark. It would even be immoral, for it would signify an abandonment of myself, a denial of my own *ego*.

Yet, on the other hand, the same person who by pure logic ought to reach the conclusion that every selfless, active love should be condemned as foolish and immoral, feels with the evidential directness of an immediate ethical experience that an egocentric, selfish, paralytic love is intolerable and repulsive. That is not what we mean when we speak of genuine love. It lacks precisely what gives genuine love its fascination, what allows us to find rest in it, what satisfies and captivates us. Its very heart, the selflessness of its devotion, has been cut out of its breast.

Are we then to say that an antinomy gapes between the logical and the psychological view of love? How is this antinomy to be reduced? How is it possible for man to love truly unselfishly without being foolish and unfaithful to his own being?

It is possible only by means of a sort of fiction whereby the lover attributes to his beloved a value which outstrips not only his own, but altogether all empirical values of a world of space and time, which transcends them all; a value, accordingly, which belongs in no wise to his own spatial world of values and can be adjusted to it; in short an absolute value, superior to the *ego*. This is the only value before which egocentric desires can and must be silent. It is that to which I am bound to surrender myself, since it is the value in every way superior to all else; it is that alone to which I can and may devote

myself with my innermost, freest assent. So in every
experience of true love there lies hidden an absolute,
or rather the assent to the sphere of the absolute,
a secret *credo in Deum*. Psychologists have therefore
described this experience of true love as an acosmic,
superterrestrial experience: for it is "not of this
world." It transcends in its essence all temporal and
spatial data of experience. It includes in its essence
the positing of an absolute. In other words: there is
no true love except a love in God. It may be that
one or other, who loves truly, knows nothing of this
absolute, of this love in God; he may even be short-
sighted enough to imagine that he acts reasonably,
when he loves selflessly, without consciously believing
in God, as the absolute value. But if his love is true
love "in deed and in truth," as St. John expresses it,
then his experience of love contains implicitly, at
least, whether he knows it or not, the positing of
God. God, His absoluteness, His infinite perfection
and lovableness, is the secret motive, the secret spring
of the energy, the secret native soil of his love. Even
some of the favourite phrases of love—like "to adore
his beloved"—indicate this fact. The lover can
reach his beloved only through God. God alone can
carry him over that dead point which lies between
the *ego* and the *alter* and cannot be transcended by
mere logic. It requires understanding and courage
to appreciate this position and to affirm one's faith
in the Absolute despite its human wrappings. As
Descartes once said: *Je pense, donc je suis*, so here it

might be said: "I love, therefore I believe." Thus in every genuine, unselfish, serious love belief in God is contained, even really presupposed. No one has expressed this truth with greater profundity than the Apostle of love, St. John, when he exhorted his disciples: "Dearly beloved, let us love one another: for charity is of God. And everyone that loveth is born of God and knoweth God."

Considered, then, even merely phenomenologically, love points towards faith. For it is only by faith that I can grasp that absolute, which love essentially includes, without which it cannot exist. When this faith in the absolute is artificially removed from the experience of love, the consequence is that love is incapable of reaching beyond the range of an earthy, crude, selfish existence and of rousing the heroism of devotion.

It is therefore symptomatic that monistic ethics, which on principle abstracts from belief in God and from any supernatural foundation, proves incapable of even theoretically maintaining a heroic morality, let alone of realising it among its followers. Why did people in the distress of the world war call so insistantly for those Sisters of Charity who draw all their love from their faith, whose love was a love for God's sake? Why do we find those heroic figures of heroic charity to whom even unbelief pays its tribute of respect, figures like St. Vincent de Paul, like Camillus de Lellis, like Don Bosco or St. Elisabeth, just there, where faith has received its purest and fullest form in dogma, its most active and exhaustive expression in cult and in life—in the Catholic Church? Is there not food for thought in the fact that even those pagan philosophers who (perhaps not uninfluenced by Christian thought, for all their fundamentally monistic attitude) for the first time seriously considered and proclaimed in pagan lands the ideal of a general love of man—for instance, the slave Epictetus—gave a strongly religious tone to their stoical speculation and combined with their profession of universal love of man also the profession of God as the Father of all things? There is only the Indian sage, Gautama Buddha, who seems to contradict this principle of an essential connexion of faith with love, so far as he formulated, as many think, a purely atheistic morality, devoid of all faith, and swore in his numerous followers upon this teaching. But apart from the fact that this assertion of the atheistic character of Buddha's ethics has met with scepticism recently, and leaving aside the fact that this irreligious ethics, even if it was actually preached, remained restricted to a small circle, while the large mass of the Buddhist faithful relapsed into a wild polytheism, it is worth while to point out that Buddha's commandment to love, his teaching of "*mettasatta*," can in no way be put on the same level as Christian charity. Kindness to animals and men (*metta*) is one of the chief commands of the Indian sage, but this kindness is something purely negative, a mere tolerating and suffering of evil, not active conduct as in Christian faith. Its object is, as Buddha expresses it, none other than to "free the soul," i.e. by non-acting on principle, by willing suffering, to stifle the thirst for life in the soul and to prepare thereby for Nirvana. Buddha's command to love is thus in the last resort conceived in terms of egoism. The purely negative, passive suffering and toleration is simply a means to self-deliverance. It lacks therefore what is just the characteristic feature of Christian charity: the selflessness of devotion, its active even vehement element, and its determined practical helpfulness.

We may then say: wherever there is true love, there is faith. Even in the Old Testament we find faith placed next to love; next to the command: "Thou shalt love thy neighbour," the other: "Thou shalt love God with thy whole heart." Even in the Old Testament there is no morality which was not at the same time religion, no love without faith. It is true that the inner connexion between faith and love was not sufficiently clearly formulated. The two commands were quoted side by side, without their overlapping and mutual dependence being fully seen. A Rabbi one day asked one of his disciples: "Which path do you see before you, when you awaken of a morning?" The disciple answered: "The path of the love of God and that of the love of my neighbour." Thereupon the Rabbi asked: "And which of these will you take first?" The disciple blushed and could not give the answer. Then the master remarked:

"The first path you are to take is that of the love of your neighbour."

It is clear then that for the Old Testament the two paths are still distinct. Hence also the question of the Rabbi. For the disciple of Christ the question has no longer any sense. For him there are not two paths; there is but the single path of salvation: the love of God and of his neighbour. They cannot be separated. Where true love of God is found, there also is true love of one's neighbour; wherever there is true faith, there also is true love. Both attitudes are merely different reactions of one and the same fundamental attitude: Love in God.

It was an original feat of Jesus to have set this internal connexion of faith and love clearly before us. As elsewhere, so here He fulfilled the Old Testament. In His own Person, the appearance of God among men, the bodily revelation of the supernatural, the mystery of faith and of love at the same time, He revealed by his subtle touch the supernatural basis of all true love on earth, rooted in the faith in the Father. There is only one true love, that which springs from faith. All true love is love in God, love for the sake of the Father.

Even a philosopher like Nietzsche was unable wholly to escape the spell of this revelation. In his work "Beyond Good and Evil" occurs the significant remark: "To love man for God's sake is, up till now, the noblest and remotest sentiment attained to among mankind. That love of man without some sort of sanctifying *arrière-pensée* is merely another foolishness and bestiality, that this propensity to love man has yet to receive from some higher tendency its measure, its refinement, its little pinch of salt and its little grain of spice—whatever man it was who first felt and experienced this, however much his speech may have blundered when it attempted to formulate anything so delicate, he must remain for us for all times sacred and worthy of reverence."

Since the time of Jesus we know that every true love lives and breathes and has its being in faith. Faith alone carries myself, my intellect, my heart out of this terrestrial microcosm, out of the limitations of purely terrestrial points of view and considerations, out of the narrow selfish desires and cares up into those altitudes where infinity opens before me, where something "quite different" shines, Divinity, Sanctity, perfect Purity. Here, in the kingdom of God, is purest reality, the Life of life, the Power of powers, the Spirit of spirits, the Value of all values. True life comes, not from below, but from above, from the Father of light. The strong impulses, the pure mind, those streams of strength that never fail, spring from there. So faith belongs to love in an essential, indissoluble bond: faith creates love, safeguards love, purifies love, strengthens love. For it gives to love that which profane love is lacking, the deep passionate breath of infinity, that characteristic tendency to superhuman greatness, that passion for heroic, incredible, unheard-of things, that foolishness of the Cross, before which all earthly pathos crumbles and breaks into dust.

Let us gather up what we said: true love can be found only where the absolute, the divine, is somehow co-involved: in other words, true love is at the same time love of God. And inasmuch as the reality of God is apprehended through faith, faith cannot be separated from true love.

This is an important conclusion. For it comes to this, that everything necessarily belonging to faith, whatever provides its foundations, its protection and usefulness, consequently the entire means of salvation of the Church, her dogma, her sacraments, her cult, her constitution, must stand in some essential relation to love. For all this serves in the last resort precisely the purpose of bringing home to us that world of God from which true love springs. Faith, in all its utterances, institutions, functions is concerned with God and His saving reality, and therefore ultimately with love, which has its roots in that reality. This applies especially to dogma. Dogma is, after all, nothing else but the glad news of the incarnation of the Word of God, the joyous fact that God's sacred reality has been revealed to us in His Son. Whatever is formulated in the individual articles of faith serves merely the all-round unfolding, the safeguarding and application of this single fundamental truth of the appearance of God upon earth. The sacraments, the cult and the priest serve that same theophany. They bring within our reach the supernatural blessings of the reality of God, manifested in Christ, and illustrate and apply it. The same theophany is served by the Pope and the bishops, by their supreme pastoral measures and decisions. Through them the kingdom of God in us becomes the kingdom of God among us, a visible community of the faithful, protected against error and safeguarded against divisions and decay. In this manner the Church proclaims and bears witness to God as the ultimate spring of all blessings by her entire essence as an institution of the means of salvation. She creates that supernatural world and that range of life saturated with divine power where true love can alone thrive. Everything about her is related to that love which overcomes the world, to the preparation and protection of that heavenly kingdom which is wholly love, "charity from a pure heart, and a good conscience, and an unfeigned faith" (*I Tim.* i, 5).

But the Church stands not only in so indirect a relation to love. Rather is she linked with love so intimately that love penetrates down into the last cells of her organism as an institution for salvation, and makes her in her essence into a wonderful revelation of love. Everything about her not merely points to love, but is born of love, steeped in love, breathing love. So dogma is in reality nothing but the joyous message of that love wherewith God first loved us, created, saved and sanctified us, the joyous message of the continuous process of the love wherewith God gave Himself to men. The sacraments are nothing but the irradiation and continuous working of this divine love in the Church and in the hearts of the faithful. The papacy and the episcopate have sprung from the love of the Saviour, an act of love towards his brethren, the service of a servant, as St. Paul expresses it. And the Church herself, sacred, immaculate, is in her deepest being the mystical Body of Christ on earth, the manifestation in time and space and the revelation of His incarnate love, the empirical completion and perfection of that last extreme act of the love of God in which He revealed Himself not only by signs and words, but gave His only Son so that we might come to the Father.

Wherever we may look in our Church, on all sides everything points to the one thing needful: "That is the first commandment: Thou shalt love the Lord thy God with thy whole heart. . . And the second is like to this: Thou shalt love thy neighbour as thyself." The entire ecclesiastical organism is not only in its ultimate purpose, but in its very essence, an urgent call to the love of God and of our neighbour, the high canticle of love ringing through the centuries and millennia. And whoever refuses obedience to this Church, to the Holy Father, to his God-given bishop, sins in the essence of his rebellious attitude against love. Whether he knows it or not, whether he wills it or not, he places the axe upon that very root from which alone love shoots up.

The last, the deepest significance of the Church upon earth is that she is the school of this love. Her

73

being as a means to salvation aims in the last resort at this. Inasmuch as she is the means to salvation, she will have fulfilled this her existence at the moment when according to the inscrutable will of God the sowing of the seeds of that love is completed. When the sign of the Son of Man will appear in the heavens, and the new heaven, the new earth and the new kingdom of the Blessed will appear in their radiance, all the functions of the Church as the means of salvation—dogma, sacraments, bishop and Pope—will drop off like the petals when the fruit ripens. Henceforth only the essential of her will remain and will shine in eternal light: the communion of love. All that which is purely the means of salvation in her is only the *signum praefigurativum*, *signum prognosticum*, something preparatory, a pointer, that will vanish at the moment when its purpose has been fulfilled. "Prophecies shall be made void, tongues shall cease, knowledge shall be destroyed. . ." Faith will pass into vision, hope will change into possession. What alone will remain is love and the communion of love, the Church of the Blessed. "For charity never falleth away" (*I Cor.* xiii, 8).

And wherever here on earth dogma, the sacraments and the Church fail to lead a soul to this love, these means to salvation have been deprived of their deepest significance. Then they are, as St. Augustine says again and again, mere external forms of piety (*formae pietatis*), lacking in the power of salvation; they are a form without content, a flower without fruit. Theology speaks of a *fides informis*, a "shapeless faith," meaning a faith atrophied and crippled in its essence because it is lacking in love. And the Church never wearies in sermon and catechism, in spiritual exercises and missions to bring home to the faithful the tremendous words of St. Paul which condemn with unparalleled force all that empty, merely external form of churchmanship, that sheer formalism: "If I should have prophecy and should know all mysteries and all knowledge, and if I should have all faith, so that I could remove mountains, and have not charity, I am nothing. And if I should distribute all my goods to feed the poor, and if I should deliver my body to be burned, and have not charity, it profiteth me nothing" (*I Cor.* xiii, 2, 3). It would be merely continuing on the lines of St. Paul to add: mere observance of the dogmas of the Church, mere obedience to the infallible Pope, mere frequent communions, participation in Church societies and organisations—all that will not do it either. Even if you do all these things, but have no charity, it will profit you nothing. "But charity is patient, is kind; charity envieth not, dealeth not perversely, is not puffed up. . . ." If you have not this charity, nothing will profit you.

If thus all and everything aims at this love and finds its ultimate significance in this love, whence comes that terrible and undeniable contrast between faith and love which we pointed out at the beginning? What is the reason why common opinion so definitely refuses to see in the faithful the natural vehicle and messenger of true love? Why is it that the intimate and essential correlation between faith and love which we have established, is by no means always visibly present in the individual Christian? And why is it that in certain periods of history the contrast between faith and love went so far that faith killed love? Why is it that we even nowadays suffer under this contrast?

A priori such a contrast is possible and thinkable because faith and love are not identical, but are only in their essences ordered towards each other. Who could deny that this contrast actually emerged and still exists? But the fault of this contrast does not lie with faith or with the Church as the foundation supporting the reality of this faith. We established the fact that whatever is in the Church, her essence and her function is born of the spirit of love and aims at love. There is nothing in the Church, neither in her dogmas nor her ritual nor her organisation, which in and by itself, by its mere existence or its special function could offer a hold or motive for hatred and dispute.

It is then out of the question that the Church herself can provide the basis of this deplorable contrast between faith and love. This basis must be sought, not in the objective, ecclesiastical factors, but in the subjective, personal factors of the situation. The fault lies, not in the Church, but in her members. And not only the lay-folk, but ecclesiastics, even

bishops and popes have been at fault. Sin is possible
wherever there is flesh and blood; it may be that
through incompetence or weakness the highest and
only purpose of all ecclesiastical life and function-
ing, namely this holy love, may be frustrated. Could
the separation of the Eastern Church have happened,
could the cleavage in the Western Church in the
sixteenth century have occurred, if the sacred commandment of love with a pure heart and unfeigned
faith had remained for all, on both sides, the supreme
and immoveable directing line of thought and action?
Every cleavage, every heresy in the Church is redu-
cible, as St. Augustine points out, to a weakening,
a failure of the spirit of love among the members of
Christ. Wherever is true love, there also is the *unitas
caritatis*, the union of love. There may be differences
of opinion and dogmatic disputes, but the union of
love will never be threatened with disruption and a
mutilation of the Body of Christ.

That same lack of love among the members of
Christ bears the responsibility, if a similar contrast
between faith and love is so acutely felt in our present
narrow, small lives. Is it not unspeakably sad that we
Catholics are no longer, as formerly, recognised by
our love, that no longer faith and love, but faith alone
is our distinguishing mark. Whose fault is it that the
old equation, Catholic Christianity = love in faith =
faith in love, applies no longer, that it cannot longer
be said as it was of the primitive faithful: "See how
they love one another"? Certainly not the fault of

the Church, who never wearies, day by day, to exhort to love and to give love, but the fault of ourselves alone, her members. Where is the Catholic who would not have to confess in this respect: *mea culpa, mea maxima culpa?*

Is it not our own fault to a very large extent that the recruiting power of our Church, which in the time of primitive Christianity had been so sweeping and victorious, has failed now for centuries so uncannily, that the riches of our faith are so largely unknown and despised, because our faith does not bear that fruit of love which should be expected of it? Why are we in the works of our love no proof of the spirit and strength in the victoriousness of the Catholic faith? Why do we rather take refuge in cheap speech and in dead books to testify to our faith, whereas the only overwhelming and effective apologia for the living reality is that of the glowing heart, of active devoted love? Should we not long ago have conquered the whole world for the joyous news of our faith, if not over wide stretches the words even now applied to us: *refrigescet caritas multorum?* The love of many is cooling! Here destiny lies in wait for us; here our responsibility stares us in the face; here our crisis awaits us and judgment threatens. For are we worthy that our Church should flourish, when our love wilts? Unless the Catholic faith kindles the spirit of love at least in our families, unless our sodalities and parishes are real centres of love—ἀγάπαι, as St. Ignatius of Antioch calls them—unless our public life is touched by the warm breath of our charity, unless every errand-boy and every charwoman is for us our brother and sister, there can be no hope of a renewal, of a deepening and expansion of Catholic life in the world. Here, at this point and no other, the decision will be reached whether Catholicism nowadays is strong enough to overcome the spirit of modern times in its inner being, to reconquer the mind of Western Europe and to carry the Gospel into all the world, as once St. Paul did in a few years, or whether it is first to lapse, according to the intentions of Divine justice and mercy, into a period of stagnation or perhaps even into the hard times of the catacombs, until its faith, purged by sorrow, shall again put forth the fruits of love.

Heavy with questions and cares, in prayer and trust we lift our eyes to him who has planted faith in our hearts and has given it the waters of love. *Veni sancte Spiritus*! Help us, o God! for indeed we know "unless the Lord build the house, they labour in vain that build it; unless the Lord keep the city, he watcheth in vain that keepeth it."

VENI, SANCTE SPIRITUS,

REPLE TUORUM CORDA FIDELIUM

ET TUI AMORIS IN EIS

IGNEM

ACCENDE

AMEN

PRINTED IN GREAT BRITAIN BY
THE   STANHOPE   PRESS   LTD
ROCHESTER   :   :   KENT